JAZZ DRUMMING
TRANSITIONS

BY TERRY O'MAHONEY

Edited by Rick Mattingly

ISBN 978-1-4234-8543-8

HAL•LEONARD®
CORPORATION
7777 W. BLUEMOUND RD. P.O. BOX 13819 MILWAUKEE, WI 53213

In Australia Contact:
Hal Leonard Australia Pty. Ltd.
4 Lentara Court
Cheltenham, Victoria, 3192 Australia
Email: ausadmin@halleonard.com.au

Visit Hal Leonard Online at
www.halleonard.com

CONTENTS

CD TRACKS

CD 1

CD 2

CD 3

PREFACE

Jazz Drumming Transitions will help any drummer prepare for the following musical challenges:

- Changing smoothly between various Afro-Cuban/Brazilian feels to a swing feel
- Becoming familiar with modern swing styles (ECM, "broken swing" feel, etc.)
- Soloing over different types of ostinatos ("vamps")
- Becoming familiar with big band chart reading in styles other than traditional swing
- Practicing "metric modulations" and tempo changes commonly found in musical situations, jam settings, or in contemporary drum charts
- Making the overall musical "transition" from traditional big band swing charts to contemporary jazz ensemble compositions
- Changing from sticks to brushes (or vice versa)
- Changing from one tempo to another (e.g., double time, metric modulation)
- Becoming familiar with modern swing timekeeping practices

Jazz has been recorded for over a hundred years. In that time, however, it has changed tremendously and has incorporated many other musical styles into its mainstream (e.g., Afro-Cuban, Brazilian). As a result, contemporary drummers are often faced with many stylistic challenges that their predecessors would never have encountered.

One frequent difference between older, traditional swing-style drum charts (e.g., those in the 1940s–70s) and today's drum charts is the juxtaposition of two (or more) very different musical styles and feels. It is common to encounter a chart that starts with a rock feel but has a swing section for horn solos. It is also common for the "A" sections of a tune with an AABA form to be played in a samba or mambo feel and the bridge (or "B" section) have a swing feel. Every drummer should be able to seamlessly change between different rhythmic styles while maintaining a consistent tempo.

Another challenge is to play the "right groove" for a tune when supplied with only a short phrase to describe what the composer/arranger wants. Phrases such as "broken 2 feel," "straight eighth," "spacy," "ECM," the vague and confusing generic term "Latin" (which could mean any number of various subgenres of Afro-Cuban, Brazilian, and other styles), and other terms mean that today's drummer needs to be a veritable "drumming history book" of styles in order to properly play a chart. Being familiar with these terms/grooves and being able to move back and forth between them easily is crucial to being a successful drummer.

The conditions I have just described are not only found in big band charts, but also in small group playing situations. Often, a drummer is handed a lead sheet (a chart that contains the melody, chord symbols, and style suggestions), so the responsibility for the proper interpretation of this chart is left almost entirely to the drummer. Chart interpretation is difficult at the best of times, but without a thorough knowledge of numerous musical styles, a drummer will be completely lost.

All of these challenges are addressed in *Jazz Drumming Transitions*.

ACKNOWLEDGEMENTS

This project would not have been possible without the help of many people. I want to extend my sincere thanks to John LaBarbera, Kevin Brunkhorst, Paul Tynan, and Chuck Marohnic for their arranging assistance.

I would also like to extend my thanks to the University of Louisville Jazz I Ensemble (John LaBarbera, director), Tim Haertel (TNT Productions), Michael Vosbein (Bosphorus Cymbals), Neil Larrivee (Vic Firth Drumsticks), Mike Tracy (University of Louisville), and Gene Smith and Dr. Steven Baldner (St. Francis Xavier University).

Tracks 1–26 feature Chuck Marohnic (piano), Chris Fitzgerald (bass), and Tim Whalen (sax). Recorded at TNT Productions by Tim Haertel (August, 2008–April, 2009).

All original compositions by Terry O'Mahoney.

ABOUT THE AUTHOR

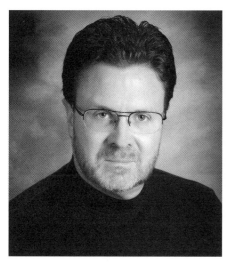

Jazz drummer Terry O'Mahoney has appeared with such jazz greats as saxophonists Bud Shank and Phil Woods, pianists James Williams and Oliver Jones, guitarists John Abercrombie and Ed Bickert, trumpeters Marvin Stamm and Terell Strafford, and trombonist Curtis Fuller, as well as performances in Japan and Brazil. His book *Motivic Drumset Soloing* was published by the Hal Leonard Corporation in 2004. He is a Professor at St. Francis Xavier University in Antigonish, Nova Scotia (Canada) where he teaches jazz and orchestral percussion, history, and coaches large and small jazz ensembles. He has performed with the Louisville Orchestra (Kentucky, USA) and Symphony Nova Scotia (Halifax). His education includes studies with jazz great Jeff Hamilton, a B.M.Ed. from the University of Louisville (Kentucky) and a Master's degree from the University of Miami (Florida). Terry's percussion ensemble compositions are published by Per-Mus Publications (Columbus, Ohio), and his articles on percussion have appeared in *Percussive Notes*, *Modern Drummer*, *Rhythm* (UK), and *Rhythm and Drums* (Japan) magazines. He was a presenter at the 2003 Percussive Arts Society International Conference (PASIC) in Louisville, Kentucky. He is a contributing editor for *Percussive Notes* magazine and is active as a clinician and adjudicator at music festivals throughout the U.S. and Canada. He endorses Bosphorus cymbals and Vic Firth drumsticks.

LEGEND

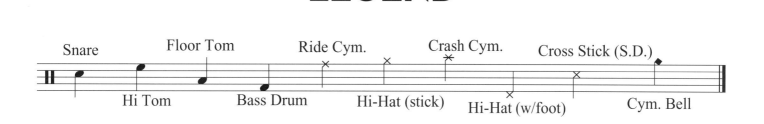

CHAPTER ONE
GROOVE TRANSITIONS

One of the first steps in working with contemporary charts is the ability to smoothly change from one feel, or groove, to another while maintaining a steady tempo. This practice of changing feels occurred in the 1940s (Dizzy Gillespie's "A Night in Tunisia"), continued in the 1950s and '60s with jazz composers such as Horace Silver ("Nica's Dream"), and is now found in many tunes. Modern arrangements often change feels, time signatures, or even tempos several times during the tune. This is often challenging because the rhythmic subdivision in one part of the tune is completely different from the part that follows it (e.g., changing from rock to swing, mambo to swing, etc.). The change from rock to swing, for example, necessitates changing from the duple-based feel of rock to the triplet-based feel of swing.

There are several things you can do to help make smooth transitions, but one of the best ways to begin practicing this concept is to maintain a consistent hi-hat pattern during the transition. For example, if you play the hi-hat on beats two and four during the swing section of a tune, it can also be played on beats two and four of the bossa nova section. In this way, the physical movement of the left foot doesn't change, thus becoming the only aspect of your playing that is the same on both sides of the transition point.

Play the following example and notice that the hi-hat does not change—but the underlying rhythmic triplet subdivision (during the swing section) *does* changes to straight eighth notes during the bossa nova section.

Example 1: (8 metronome clicks to start)

CD 1, Track 1

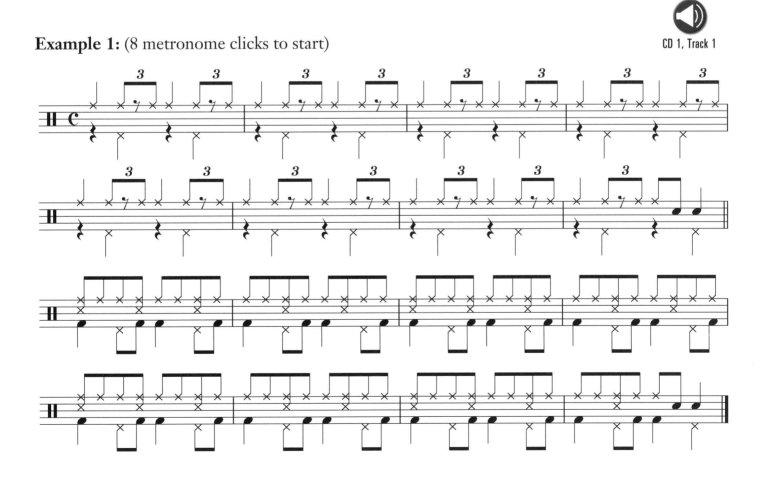

Using the hi-hat as the "pivot point" between different feels is the first step to being able to change feels without altering the tempo. After you become comfortable doing this, you can omit the hi-hat during the transition, if you wish.

Practice the following exercises that change from one feel to the other. You may use fills as "connecting material" between the two feels and also to signal to the rest of the musicians that a change of feel is imminent. Simply changing from one feel to another without any musical "warning" (i.e., a fill) can make the transition seem abrupt. When changing from a straight eighth-note feel (e.g. rock) to a swing feel, drummers often use a triplet-based swing fill in the *last bar before the transition to the swing feel.* This conveys to the rest of the band that a change is about to occur. The reverse is also true: when making the transition back to a rock feel from a swing feel, a *straight eighth-note rock-type fill in the last bar of the rock section* will signal the change back to rock. Using fills to prepare the band for feel changes has several benefits: it outlines the form of the song, helps the other musicians keep their place in the form of the tune, and prepares them to rhythmically change how they approach their improvisation.

Depending upon the situation, I often use a fill that ends on the "and" of beat four of the transition bar when changing into a swing feel. I do this when changing from a straight eighth-note feel to a swing feel so that the two different sections don't sound so musically rigid or "squared off." Another reason for this phrasing choice is that most swing music relies on the accentuation of the upbeats (such as the "and" of beat four in each measure) to propel the music and give it a sense of forward motion.

Examples 2–13 are practice vamps (without melodies) that change from one feel to another. Each track (with drums) will be followed by an identical track without drums, so you can practice making the transition from each style to swing and back again.

I used a very basic groove for Example 2. You may choose to alter the rock groove when you practice Example 2.

CD 1, Track 2/3

Example 2: Rock to Swing

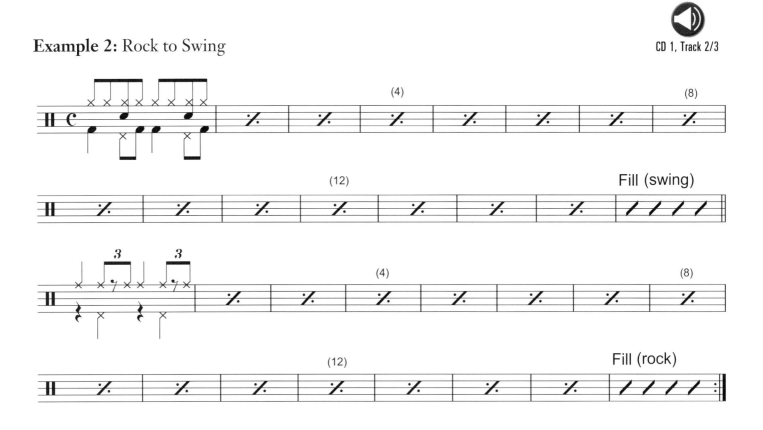

Example 3: Bossa Nova to Swing

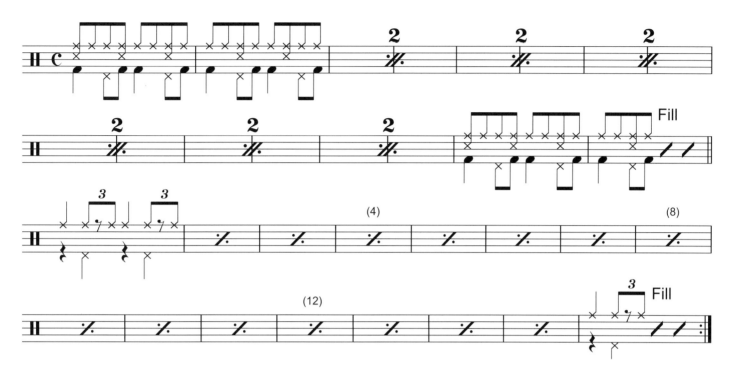

Example 4: Samba to Swing

CD 1, Track 8/9

Example 5: Mambo to Swing

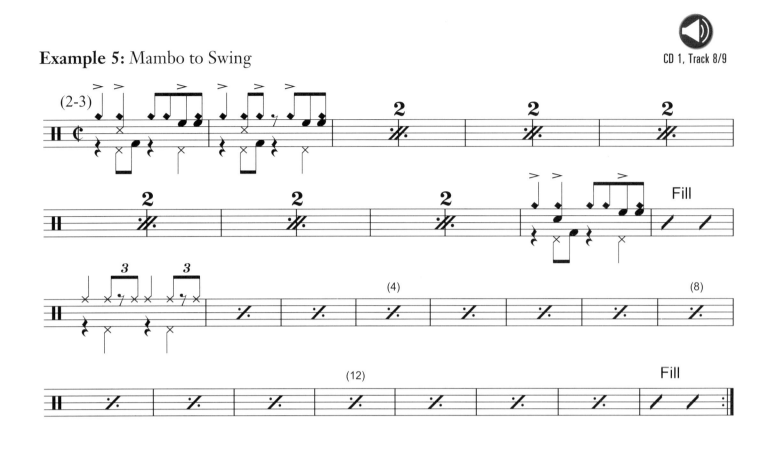

CD 1, Track 10/11

Example 6: Songo to Swing

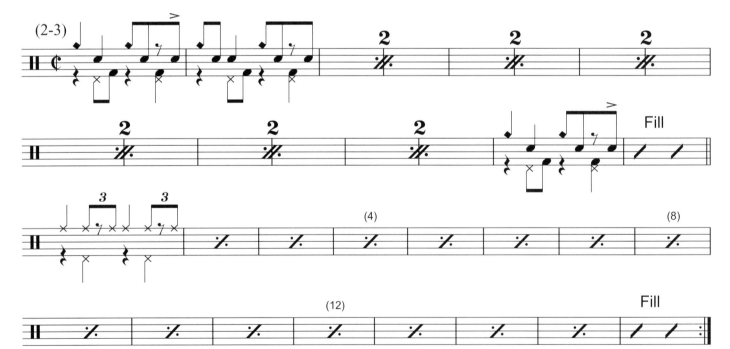

CD 1, Track 12/13

Example 7: Mozambique to Swing

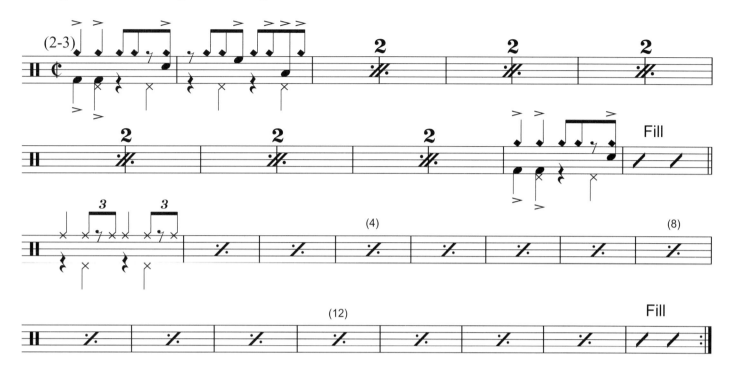

Example 8 requires some explanation. Listen to the example several times (perhaps even while tapping your foot) to understand how the pulse in the Afro-Cuban 6/8 section relates to the pulse in the swing section. The *dotted-quarter-note pulse* found in the 6/8 section is the same as the *quarter-note pulse* in the swing section. At first, this might feel like the swing slows down, but it does not. Listen to how the hi-hat part in the Afro-Cuban 6/8 section is the *same tempo* as in the swing section, except that the hi-hat is played half as often (on beats two and four) in the swing section.

Example 8A shows how the pulses relate to one another. The arrows represent the underlying pulse, and this pulse does *not* change throughout the example. What does change is what is played on top of the pulse. The arrows *before* the double bar show where the pulse occurs and are the *same tempo* as the arrows after the double bar.

Example 8A

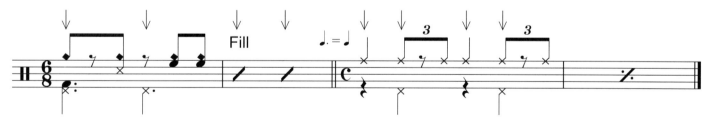

CD 1, Track 14/15

Example 8: Afro 6/8 to Swing

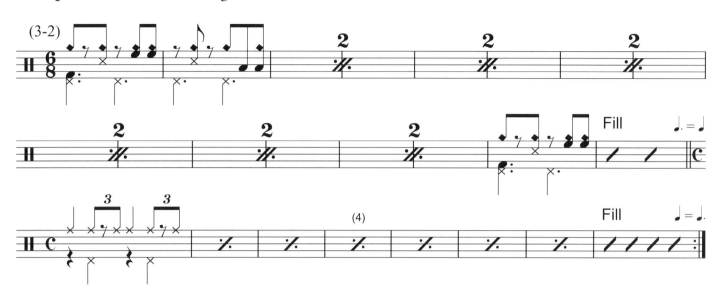

Example 9 is the same tune as Example 8. The difference between the two lies in the relationship of the pulse in the Afro-Cuban 6/8 section and the swing section. Listen to the example several times (perhaps even while tapping your foot) to understand how the pulse in the Afro-Cuban 6/8 section relates to the pulse in the swing section. In Example 9, the *dotted-quarter-note pulse* in the Afro-Cuban 6/8 section equals the *half-note pulse* in the swing section. At first, this might seem like the swing section speeds up, but it does not.

Example 9A illustrates how the two pulses relate to one another in Example 9. The arrows represent the underlying pulse, and this pulse does *not* change throughout the example. What *does* change is what is played on top of the pulse. The arrows *before* the double bar show where the pulse occurs and are the same tempo as the arrows *after* the double bar. Listen to the example several times to get acclimated to the relationship between the two sections.

Example 9A

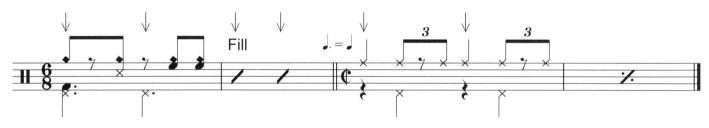

When played in this way, the swing section is often called a "double-time swing" section. In fact, arrangers sometimes write "double time" or something similar over the first bar of the swing section to indicate they want the swing section to be played this fast.

Example 9: Afro 6/8 to Double-Time Swing

CD 1, Track 16/17

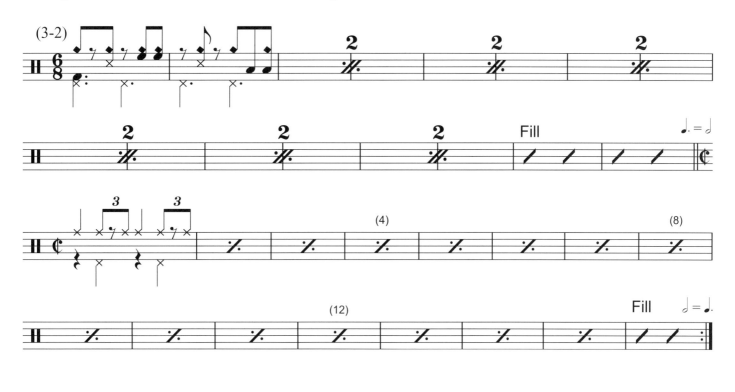

Example 10: Guaguanco to Swing

CD 1, Track 18/19

Example 11 consists of a straight-eighth-note feel changing to a swing feel. This style is often referred to as a "straight-eighth-note feel" or an "ECM groove." This feel is *not* a specific traditional folkloric pattern (e.g., Afro-Cuban, Brazilian, etc.) but a description of a style typified by drummers such as Jack DeJohnette, Jan Christiansen, and others who played on some important recordings beginning in the 1970s. These recordings were often on the European ECM label, and the style became known as the ECM style. These artists often recorded tunes that used the straight-eighth note as the underlying subdivision of their music, as opposed to the traditional triplet-based swing feel. The style is best defined by non-repetitive, ever-changing ride cymbal, hi-hat, and bass drum patterns. (See the *Recommended Listening* appendix for important ECM-style recordings.) The drumming approach in this style relies on generating a pulse with the *entire drumset*, not just one or two limbs (e.g., ride cymbal and hi-hat). Listen to how this track differs from the previous ones in this respect.

The rhythms on top of the staff represent rhythmic figures played by the piano and bass.
Try to accentuate these important rhythms with cymbal crashes or drum accents.

Example 11: Straight-Eighth (ECM) Style to Swing

CD 1, Track 20/21

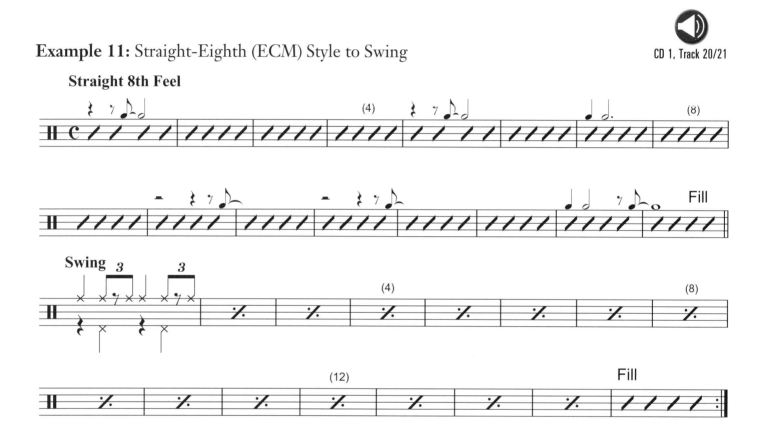

Example 12 does not change from a straight-eighth-note feel to swing (as in the previous examples), but it does change from a swing "4" feel (with the bass player playing four quarter notes per bar and the drummer playing the traditional jazz ride cymbal pattern) to a "pedal point" section. Pedal point sections are frequently just called a "pedal." During a pedal, the bass player stops playing four quarter notes per bar and plays some type of repetitive rhythmic figure that creates the illusion that the pulse has been somewhat suspended momentarily. (The pulse does not stop and the tempo remains the same.)

A pedal is often employed to create variety in the rhythmic feel. Often, the drums will play a rhythmic pattern similar to the bass rhythm (often on cymbals). I often "splash" the hi-hat cymbals together using a stomping motion on the hi-hat pedal. This creates a contrast from the tight, closed sound I play on the hi-hat during the regular "4 feel" sections of the tune. Notice how the drums return to playing the regular jazz ride pattern following the pedal section. Example 12 demonstrates a standard pedal rhythm, where the bass player plays long beats on beats two and four of each bar. The last four bars of the example demonstrate a common variation on a pedal rhythm. The bass player could also choose to do a different rhythm. When this occurs, it is probably best to imitate the bassist's rhythm.

Example 12: Swing tune with Pedal Point section

CD 1, Track 22/23

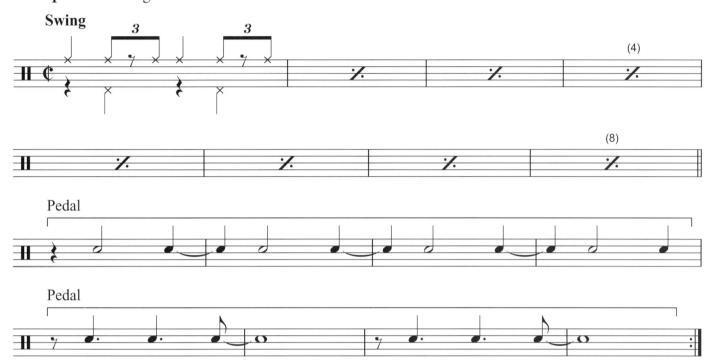

Example 13 contains a transition that occurs in Afro-Cuban music. Often, a tune will begin in an Afro-Cuban 6/8 feel but change to a more traditional straight-eighth-note mambo pattern in cut-time (2/2). The underlying pulse stays the same; the dotted-quarter-note pulse in the Afro-Cuban 6/8 *equals* the half-note pulse in the cut-time mambo.

Example 13: Afro-Cuban 6/8 to Mambo

CD 1, Track 24/25

CHAPTER TWO
CHARTS AND LEAD SHEETS

The following charts/lead sheets are examples of what you might encounter in many musical situations. Each lead sheet presents a different musical challenge, which will be discussed in the analysis before each tune. Each track will be played twice, first with drums, then without drums. Your interpretation will not be exactly the same as mine (which is the beauty of music), but it should be somewhat similar. Remember that these are example charts, and if composers or bandleaders asked you to play them differently, you'd probably want to accommodate their request!

A tune often begins with one groove, and during the improvisation section, the soloist or the chart might indicate a change of feel through their choice of rhythms or note density. This is often not discussed beforehand, so you have to be ready to change feels if the soloist indicates it. Listen to some of the following examples in which the improvisation section begins with one feel but changes as the solo progresses. Normally, the tune returns to the original feel (or combination of feels) when restating the melody at the end of the tune.

Just as in Chapter One, I often signal the change from one feel to another with a fill.

When presented with a lead sheet instead of an actual drum chart, drummers are required to "interpret" the music on the drums. This means you must play the appropriate style indicated on the chart (swing, funk, rock, Afro-Cuba, Brazilian, etc.), try to highlight important rhythms or accents found in the melody (perhaps with a snare accent or crash cymbal), or prepare an important rhythmic figure by playing a fill before the figure (also known as "setting up a figure"). These are all good ways to make the tune more interesting and musical.

Often, a tune lends itself to a drum solo over a vamp (or "ostinato"). These vamps are usually created spontaneously by the other members of the band, and the drummer is signaled by other band members to solo while the other musicians play the vamp. On other occasions, drummers solo over the entire form of the tune or just a section of a tune. Many of the examples in Chapter Two contain either a drum solo over a vamp or a solo over part (or complete form) of the tune. Following each play-along track without drums, there are vamps or entire forms of the tune that can be used to practice soloing exactly like the approach used in each tune.

Finally, the drummer must be familiar with, *and able to execute*, all of the different styles and rhythmic patterns found in today's music. By the time you *need* to play a samba in a rehearsal, it is too late to learn it! Check the *Recommended Books* appendix for a list of material that will be helpful in learning a variety of different styles and approaches you must master *before* you get to a rehearsal or performance.

ROCK TO SWING

Example 14

Format:
Melody (16 bars rock feel)
Sax solo (16 bars rock, 16 bars swing)
Piano solo (16 bars rock, 16 bars swing)
Drum solo over rock vamp (16 bars)
Melody (16 bars rock feel)

You may use Example 14A to practice soloing over a rock vamp:

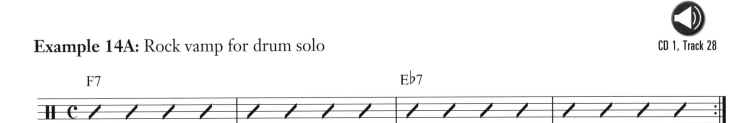

Example 14A: Rock vamp for drum solo

In Example 14, I base my solo around the rhythm of the piano and bass vamp. You may want to use a different approach and solo using other ideas or concepts.

FUNK TO SWING

In Example 15, the funk section is played in a "half time feel," during which I play variations of this basic groove during the funk sections:

Example 15: Funk to Swing

CD 1, Track 29/30

Funk

Format:

4-bar Introduction vamp (played twice, 8 bars funk feel)

Melody (16 bars funk feel, 8 bars swing feel, 16 bars funk feel)

Sax solo (16 bars funk feel)

Piano solo (8 bars swing feel, 16 bars funk feel)

Drum solo over a funk vamp (32 bars)

Melody (16 bars funk feel, 8 bars swing feel, 16 bars funk feel, end at Fine)

Example 15A: Funk vamp for drum solo

CD 1, Track 31

BOSSA NOVA TO SWING

I use variations of this basic bossa nova pattern in Example 16.

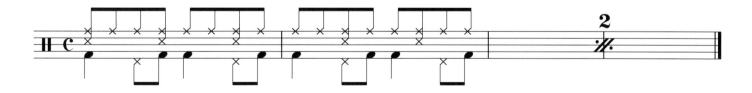

Example 16: Bossa Nova to Swing

CD 1, Track 32/33

Intro

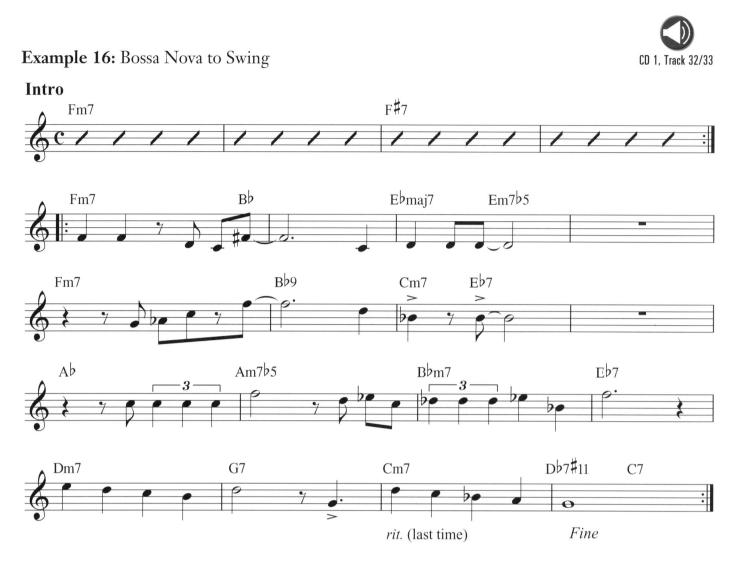

Format:

4-bar Introduction vamp (played twice, 8 bars bossa nova feel)

Melody (16 bars bossa nova feel)

Sax Solo (16 bars bossa nova feel, 16 bars swing feel)

Piano solo (16 bars bossa nova feel, 16 bars swing feel)

Drum solo over bossa nova vamp (16 bars)

Melody (16 bars bossa nova feel with a ritard to Fine)

Example 16A: Bossa Nova vamp for drum solo

CD 1, Track 34

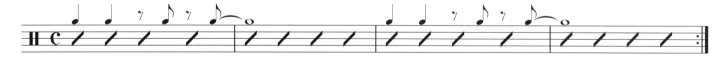

SAMBA TO SWING

Variations of this groove are used in the samba sections of Example 17:

Example 17: Samba to Swing

CD 1, Track 35/36

Format:

4-bar Introduction vamp (played twice, 8 bars samba feel)

Melody (32 bars: 16 bars samba feel, 16 bars swing feel)

Sax Solo (16 bars swing feel, 16 bars swing feel)

Piano solo (16 bars samba feel, 16 bars swing feel)

Drum solo over samba vamp (16 bars)

Melody (16 bars samba, 16 bars swing feel, end at Fine)

Example 17A: Samba vamp for drum solo

CD 1, Track 37

MAMBO TO SWING

Example 18 uses variations of this basic groove during the mambo sections:

Example 18: Mambo to Swing

CD 1, Track 38/39

Format:
4-bar Introduction vamp (played twice, 8 bars mambo feel)
Melody (32 bars mambo feel)
Sax Solo (16 bars mambo feel, 16 bars swing feel)
Piano solo (16 bars mambo feel, 16 bars swing feel)
Drum solo over mambo vamp (32 bars)
Melody (30 bars, end on Fine)

Example 18A: Mambo vamp for drum solo

CD 1, Track 40

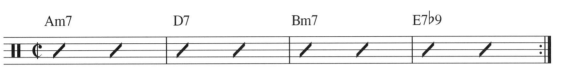

SONGO TO SWING

Example 19 uses variations of this basic songo groove:

Example 19: Songo to Swing

Intro

Fine

Format:

4-bar Introduction vamp (played twice, 8 bars songo feel)

Melody (32 bars songo feel)

Sax Solo (16 bars songo feel, 16 bars swing feel)

Piano solo (16 bars songo feel, 16 bars swing feel)

Drum solo over songo vamp (32 bars)

Melody (31 measures, end at Fine)

Example 19A: Songo vamp for drum solo

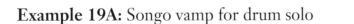

AFRO-CUBAN 6/8 TO SWING

Example 20 uses this Afro-Cuban 6/8 groove:

Example 20: Afro-Cuban 6/8 to Swing

CD 2, Track 4/5

Format:

4-bar Introduction vamp (played 4 times, 16 bars 6/8 feel)

Melody (24 bars 6/8 feel)

Piano Solo (24 bars 6/8 feel, 12 bars 4/4 swing [24 bars 2/4 swing])

Sax solo (24 bars 6/8 feel, 12 bars 4/4 swing [24 bars 2/4 swing])

Drum solo over 6/8 vamp (32 bars 2/4)

Melody (24 bars 6/8 feel, then vamp on 4-bar Introduction section, end at Fine)

Notice that in Example 19, the melody is 24 bars long. During the improvisation section, you will play 24 bars of the 6/8 feel but only *12 bars of the 4/4 swing feel* (because the 6/8 feel only has two pulses per bar and the 4/4 swing section has four pulses per bar). Another way to conceptualize this is to think that you would play 24 bars of 2/4 swing during the improvisation section.

CD 2, Track 6

Example 20A: Afro-Cuban 6/8 vamp for drum solo

(Bass line)

JAZZ WALTZ

Example 21 is a jazz waltz with two *metric modulations* taking place during the improvisation sections. A *metric modulation* is a tempo change that occurs between two different tempos in which a note value in the first tempo is equivalent to a specific note value in the second tempo. Metric modulations can occur spontaneously during jazz improvisation sections and are another way to create variety in rhythm section accompaniment techniques.

In Example 21, the first metric modulation occurs prior to the second chorus of the piano solo. The first chorus (32 bars) of this solo is in a 3/4 jazz waltz feel, but two bars before the beginning of the second piano chorus, the rhythm section begins to imply the dotted-quarter note as a "target" pulse. The dotted-quarter-note tempo (or pulse) in the first piano solo chorus becomes equivalent to the quarter-note pulse in the second piano chorus. After establishing the dotted-quarter note as the "target pulse," I begin to superimpose the jazz ride cymbal pattern against this new pulse. The arrows indicate the same underlying pulse and how the "original" and "target" pulses relate to one another. This example shows how it looks if it were notated:

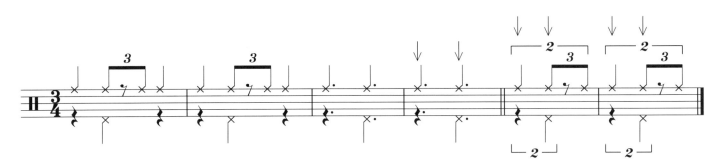

In the last four bars of the second piano chorus (using the "implied quarter-note pulse" swing feel), the rhythm section returns to the regular 3/4 jazz waltz feel.

The second example of metric modulation occurs during the second saxophone solo chorus (which follows the piano solo). The first chorus (32 bars) of the sax solo is in a traditional jazz waltz feel, with the bass playing primarily on beat one of each bar. Two bars before the beginning of the saxophone's second chorus, the rhythm section begins to imply a quadtuplet (the "grouping" of four notes found in measure 3 of the following example), thus establishing this as the "new pulse." The rhythm section then superimposes a whole measure of 4/4 jazz time in this new pulse (measure 5). The arrows indicate the placement of the musical pulse and how the "old" and "new" pulses relate to one another. This superimposed tempo continues for 30 bars of the sax solo. This is how it looks if notated:

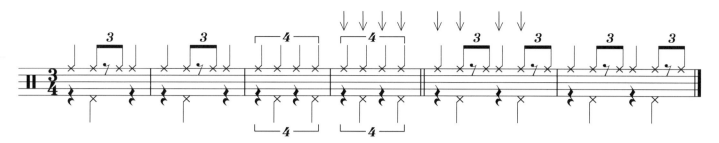

Four bars before the end of the saxophone's second solo chorus, the rhythm section begins to re-establish the original 3/4 pulse and plays the melody for the last time in the original jazz waltz feel.

These "transitions" to a new sense of pulse are commonly done by jazz groups, often spontaneously during improvisation sections. Practice this track, and when you hear a soloist implying a new pulse, this is how you can make the metric change.

Example 21: Jazz Waltz

CD 2, Track 7/8

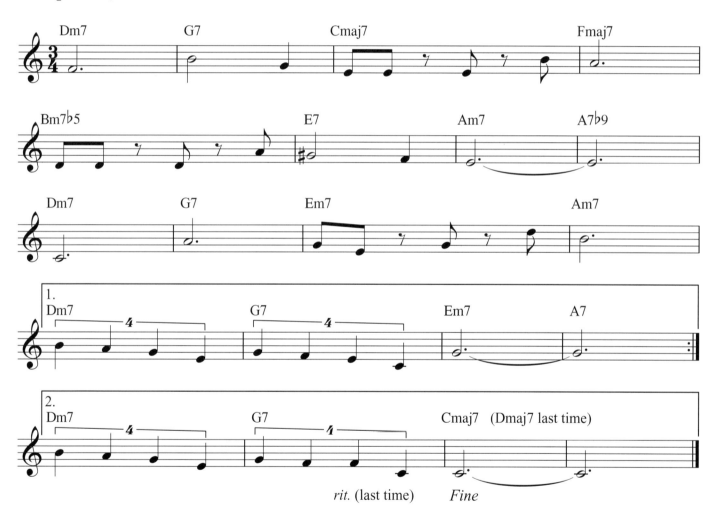

rit. (last time)   *Fine*

Format:
Melody (32 bars, jazz waltz feel)
Piano solo (32 bars waltz feel, 32 bars 2/4 swing in superimposed "two feel")
Sax solo (32 bars waltz feel, 32 bars 4/4 swing in superimposed "four feel")
Drum solo (32 bars jazz waltz over the form of the tune)
Melody (31 measures, *ritard to Fine*)

Another common performance practice is for the drummer to solo over the entire form of a tune while the rhythm section "comps" the chords. This is what I did in this tune.

CD 2, Track 9

One chorus (32 bars) of the waltz form for drum solo

A word of warning: Successfully executing metric modulations takes practice and should not be done spontaneously during a performance with players who are under-rehearsed or who do not have any experience with this technique. You should also never "force" a soloist into a metric modulation; the solo should indicate whether or not the soloist wishes to modulate.

STRAIGHT-EIGHTH NOTE ("ECM FEEL") TO SWING

Example 22 uses a straight-eighth-note "ECM" feel, on which I play non-repetitive cymbal, hi-hat, bass drum, and snare drum patterns to create an overall "time flow" with the drums. Some people refer to this as "playing broken time" or "breaking up the time." (This approach to timekeeping was discussed and demonstrated in Example 11.) Such drummers as Tony Williams, Jack DeJohnette, and Paul Motian began using this approach in the 1960s, and almost all jazz drummers today (unless they are specifically trying to emulate the traditional bebop drumming style of Max Roach, Art Blakey, Philly Joe Jones, etc.) vary their ride cymbal pattern in some way. This is a huge departure from playing repeated rhythmic patterns in any one limb, which is how most jazz until the 1960s, as well as rock and funk, was usually played.

Unlike most Afro-Cuban or Brazilian rhythmic patterns (e.g., mambo, bossa nova), there is no generic "ECM drumset pattern" that can be applied to all tunes that require an ECM/straight-eighth-note feel. The only way to learn this style is by listening, analyzing recordings, and emulating drummers who play in this style. Jan Christensen is one of the most important drummers in the ECM school of drumming. Listen to his playing on "Oceanus," "Drifting Pedals," and "Nimbus" on Ralph Towner's *Solstice* CD, or Tony Williams on "Maiden Voyage" on Herbie Hancock's *Maiden Voyage* CD.

Listen to how I try to accent the melody with my cymbals or other parts of the drumset and how I use the snare, bass, and toms to "fill in" the space between important rhythm points in the melody or during the solos. This is an integral part of the modern "ECM" or "broken time" style. Subtle use of dynamics is also very important when playing the ECM style. I try to follow a soloist's dynamics more closely in this style than in some other jazz styles.

During the swing section, I vary my hi-hat and ride rhythms more than in traditional swing tunes. I also use the shoulder of the stick on the bow of the cymbal to create subtle accents and changes of timbre while keeping time. As a soloist "builds" the solo, I usually become more rhythmically active on the drums. This is another way to create a sense of variety and intensity in the area of rhythm-section accompaniment. My solo employs subtle dynamics and is rhythmically based around the vamp figure played by the bass and piano.

Example 22: Straight-Eighth-Note ("ECM feel") to Swing

CD 2, Track 10/11

Intro

Format:

4-bar Introduction vamp (played twice, 8 bars straight-eighth-note feel)

Melody (32 bars, straight-eighth-note feel)

Piano solo (32 bars straight-eighth feel, 32 bars swing feel)

Sax solo (32 bars straight-eighth-feel, 32 bars swing feel)

Drum solo over 4-bar straight-eighth-note introduction vamp (16 bars)

Melody (32 bars straight-eighth-feel, end on introduction vamp for 15 bars)

Example 22A: "ECM" vamp for drum solo   CD 1, Track 12

BLUESY NEW ORLEANS "SECOND LINE" FEEL TO SWING

Example 23 is a funky "New Orleans second line" inspired jazz track. It has been included not so much for its transition to a traditional swing (although this happens once during this example) but as a specific jazz style study. This style is occasionally applied to a medium-slow swing tune, and it is important to be familiar with it before someone asks you to play like this. It has a slow New Orleans second-line swing "march feel" that is played primarily on the snare drum. Notice how I rhythmically "quote the melody" at different points in the melody (e.g., measure 7–8, 15–16, and 31–32). Drummer Bill Stewart's performance on the first part of "Hammock Soliloquy" (John Scofield's *EnRoute[Live]* CD) is an example of this style, as well as Jeff Watts on "Rhythm in Blue Suite: Playground" from Danilo Perez's *Central Avenue* CD.

Example 23: Bluesy New Orleans "Second Line" Feel to Swing

CD 2, Track 13/14

Format:

Melody (32 bars, New Orleans "second line" feel)

Guitar solo (16 bars "second line feel, 8 bars swing feel, 8 bars "second line" feel)

Drum solo over "second line" vamp (16 bars)

Melody (played from measure 17–32, end on short note at *Fine*)

Although I only solo on 16 bars of the melody in Example 23, you can practice soloing over the whole form of the tune using Track 14 on CD 2 (without drums).

MODERN "2" SWING FEEL TO "4" FEEL

Example 24 is a tune that changes from a modern "broken 2" ride pattern to a straight-ahead traditional "4 feel" during the solos. The modern "broken 2" feel is characterized by a spacious ride cymbal pattern and often accents the upbeats before beats 1 and 3 rather than beats 2 and 4. Listen to the ride cymbal patterns during the "2 feel" sections; they often correspond to the rhythm of the bass part.

An example of a "broken 2" swing feel played by Jack DeJohnette can be heard on "The Masquerade Is Over" on the Keith Jarrett Trio CD *Standards*, Vol. 1.

Example 24: Modern "2" Swing Feel to "4" Feel   CD 2, Track 15/16

Format:
Melody (16 bars "2" feel)
Sax solo (16 bars "2" feel, 16 bars "4" feel)
Piano solo (16 bars "2" feel, 16 bars "4" feel)
Drum solo over the form of the tune twice (32 bars)
Melody (15 bars, end at *Fine*)

I solo for two choruses over the 16-bar form of the tune in Example 24. I often use the rhythm of the chord progression as a "rhythmic framework" of my solos by basing my fills and accents around accented chords (e.g., measures 6, 10, and 13). This can be effective at slower tempos or when you want to correlate your solo to the form of a tune.

CD 2, Track 17

Two choruses of Example 24 for drum solo

BALLAD

Example 25 is an example of playing in a loose, "textural" way vs. "strictly keeping time." This example is a ballad in which the melody is played "out of time" (*rubato*) the first time. Elvin Jones uses this approach on the tune "Psalm" on John Coltrane's *A Love Supreme* CD.

The track begins with 8 clicks; this is to signal the start of the tune, not to indicate the tempo. I used timpani mallets on the drums to create a different, sustained-type of texture during the first statement of the melody. This approach works well when the tempo is subject to the interpretation of the lead voice (in this case, the saxophone). Notice that I don't always "land on the beat" precisely with the other musicians; this is typical of playing in a loose, more musically free musical situation. Do not be overly concerned with trying to play exactly how I played when practicing with the track. When you can "sense" when the other musicians are going to play something, then you will have achieved the goal of this exercise. The point of playing this way is not to achieve perfect synchronization with the other musicians, but to create an overall flowing mood and different texture from the drums using soft timpani mallets.

Try to *generally* follow the pulse the other musicians set up. I usually try to place a cymbal crash at important points in the melody (e.g., on the downbeat of a new section); this often helps keep the band musically together. I turn the snares off and think of the snare drum as another tom in this style. The drum part is supposed to sound like waves crashing on the shore, or some other rumbling, organic texture—not the time reference for the other musicians. When performing this style live, whoever is playing the melody will often "conduct" the pulse with his or her instrument or head, so the tune actually may have a pulse, just not a consistent one.

In Example 25, the piano establishes a steady tempo after the first statement of the melody. The piano then plays a solo in a loose "2" feel (with a half-note pulse), so I switch to brushes. (Playing with sticks would also work here.) I play the brushes is a loose, interactive way in this style, using hi-hat "splashes," cymbal/hi-hat rolls, and other rhythmic fills to create a sense of pulse. The saxophonist solos for 24 bars (3/4 of the form of the tune), finishes the solo with a slight *ritard*, and then restates the last 8 bars of the melody to conclude the tune. I switch back to timpani mallets for the last 8 bars of the tune because the tempo is being played *rubato* again.

Paul Motian and Elvin Jones were some of the first jazz drummers to play brushes in this way. Listen to recordings of Motian with the Bill Evans Trio or Jones with the John Coltrane Quartet in the 1960s.

I did not solo in Example 25, although drum solos are done in this style. Often, drum solos are performed completely *rubato*, frequently using timpani mallets. Many solos heard in this style are open-ended "drum features" in which the drummer will play for an extended period of time and then signal the other musicians when he or she wants to return to the melody. Soloing in this style is liberating because almost anything a drummer wants to do is acceptable. You may choose to play in tempo, out of tempo, with sticks, with brushes, with mallets, or even with your hands.

CD 2, Track 18/19

Example 25: Ballad

Fine

Format:

Melody (32 bars *rubato* with timpani mallets)

Piano solo (32 bars in tempo with brushes)

Sax solo (24 bars with a *ritard* in the last 2 bars)

Sax plays the last 8 bars of the melody (*rubato* with mallets, *ritard* to *Fine*).

"SOUL JAZZ"

Example 26 is a funky, "soul jazz" track. This groove works well with a vamp-oriented tune where you want to have a strong rhythmic foundation for a tune and want to provide something different from the standard jazz groove. The strength of the groove is rooted in the repetition of the snare/tom pattern throughout the tune. I turned the snares off during the "soul jazz" section to give the groove an earthier, more organic feel. I turned the snares back on during the swing sections. Tony Williams' tune "Sister Cheryl," which can be found on Wynton Marsalis' self-titled CD, is similar to this groove.

This is the basic pattern I used during the "soul jazz" sections of the tune:

Example 26: "Soul Jazz" groove to swing

CD 2, Track 20/21

Format:
4-bar Introduction vamp (32 bars)
Melody twice (32 bars soul-jazz feel)
Sax solo (16 bars soul jazz, 16 bars swing)
Piano solo (16 bars soul jazz, 16 bars swing)
Drum solo (32 bars over soul-jazz vamp)
Melody (played twice, 32 bars soul-jazz feel)
Ending (Introduction vamp, 18 times)

My solo over the vamp was often more "time based" than strictly soloistic. This means I played ideas that often sounded like fills and time rather than just solo ideas around the drumset. I also tried to rhythmically base my solo around the rhythm of the vamp figure.

Example 26A: "Soul Jazz" vamp for drum solo

CD 2, Track 22

CHAPTER THREE
ORIGINAL TUNES

This chapter deals with charts (big band or small group) that one might encounter in college or the professional world. These charts are based on jazz styles that developed after the standard big band swing styles of Count Basie, Duke Ellington, and others.

It will help if you already understand how to approach traditional big band swing charts, and you should be comfortable "setting up" ensemble figures (played by the entire band in unison) and interpreting background figures (played by a limited number of players in support of a soloist). Many fine books address this subject (see the *Recommended Books* appendix).

Although the examples heard here employ a big band, charts can be written for any size ensemble. Drum charts are most often used for ensembles that involve horns, specific arrangements, background figures, etc. Each chart in this chapter was written to demonstrate either a particular style of music or present a musical challenge not normally encountered in traditional swing/Latin/rock charts found in most high schools and colleges. Each chart and its musical considerations and challenges will be discussed in the *Chart Analysis* found immediately before each chart.

It is important to note that there is no *absolute* standard way of notating big band drum charts. Each writer seems to have a different way of indicating what he or she wants the drummer to play and/or what is taking place in the chart. Deciphering what is happening in the chart and making musical decisions based on extensive listening, analysis of other drummers and their playing styles, and understanding what is stylistically appropriate to play is what's meant by "interpreting the drum chart." If you haven't heard, or don't understand what is meant by the term "straight-eighth-note feel," then it will be impossible to play a chart that is written in that style.

Another problem with chart terminology is something I refer to as "hybrid genre terms." Examples of this include such terms as *funk samba*, *greasy blues*, *spacy jazz*, *swing bossa nova*, *Latin rock*, *quasi-Latin rock*, *swing funk*, etc. When confronted with such terms, drummers often create some combination of the two genres to try to satisfy the composer's request. For example, a funk samba might have a dotted-eighth/sixteenth-note bass drum pattern (from samba) with a backbeat on beats 2 and 4 (from funk). There is no definitive pattern for this situation, so being familiar with as many genres as possible will allow you to create a "hybrid groove" if the need arises.

The important thing to remember is that there are basically two types of rhythmic figures written in a big band drum chart: background figures and ensemble figures.

Background figures are the musical phrases played by members of the band while someone is soloing. Musically, when someone is soloing, that is the focus of the tune. Background figures are a secondary consideration and can be integrated into the timekeeping.

Ensemble figures are rhythmic phrases played by a section or entire band in unison. As a rule, these need some type of fill that precedes the rhythmic figure to help cue the band's entrance.

Notation

I use a variety of notational approaches in order to demonstrate how different writers use different symbols to indicate various ways to approach the chart.

Slashes *in the staff* normally indicate to play the appropriate feel for the tune as indicated at the beginning of the chart or by the bandleader:

Bossa Nova

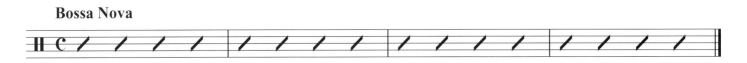

Notation with figures written above the staff usually indicates background figures (almost always when a solo is taking place simultaneously), but may mean ensemble figures if the dynamic is loud.

Figures written in the staff normally represent full ensemble figures:

"Rhythmic (slash) notation" is used by some composers to indicate full ensemble figures:

"PARTY AT EWR"

Chart Analysis

"Party at EWR" is a medium-tempo 4/4 swing tune based on a four-bar modal vamp. Modal vamp-based tunes gained prominence in the jazz world in the late 1950s and '60s. Many modal tunes are a collection of short, easily remembered melodic fragments that are often transposed into several different keys to build a complete composition.

The vamp figure serves as the basis of the introduction (measures 1–16). I "set up" the band's entrances on the "and" of beat one of the vamp figure with a snare drum note on beat 1 (mm. 1, 5, 9, 12) and play "soloistic time" for the last three bars of the vamp figure. I interpret "soloistic time" to mean playing the ride cymbal pattern while adding comping figures and fills with snare drum and bass drum.

This chart uses a 32-bar AABA melodic form. The melody begins at Letter A, so I focus on playing time as well as setting up the vamp figure when it appears every four bars. At Letter B, there is a soft "pedal section," which means to give the impression that the time is suspended momentarily. I imply this by splashing the hi-hat and playing the ride on beats 2 and 4. The melody returns again at measure 41 for eight bars, and I approach this section the same way as the first eight measures of the tune.

Letter C is a 32-bar tenor sax/drum duet. The challenge in this type of setting is to maintain the tempo by basing your timekeeping on the ride cymbal, yet interact with the tenor player by adding interesting snare drum/bass drum comping figures and fills.

After the duet at Letter C, turn your attention back to the entire band as they enter with background figures while the tenor sax solo continues through Letter E.

Letter F is a drum solo with rhythmic accompaniment figures played by the band. The challenge here is to play a cohesive solo that integrates these figures successfully. I often begin these types of solos by clearly "setting up" each band figure with some sort of obvious fill and then slowly moving away from the figures and only playing selected sections of them.

The melody returns at Letter H, and I approach it the same way as the original melody by playing time (with the exception of the pedal section and coda section from Letter J to the end). A short coda section begins in measure 149 with a pedal section for four bars, followed by four bars of a drum fill underneath sustained chords by the band. The tune ends with two short eighth notes on beat 1 of the final bar (which I play on the snare drum).

An example of this style of modal tune is Cedar Walton's "Firm Roots" on Clifford Jordan's *Firm Roots* CD.

Example 27A: Use this excerpt to practice the saxophone/drum duet at Letter C.
This excerpt includes the metronome track, but the complete play-along track does not.

CD 3, Track 1

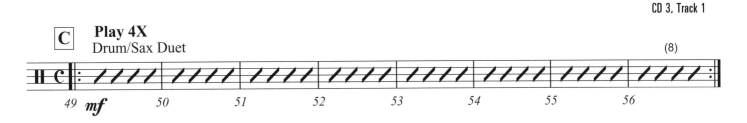

Example 27B: Use this excerpt from the chart to practice soloing over the rhythmic figures between Letters F and H. The example begins four bars before letter F. This excerpt includes the metronome track but the play-along track does not.

CD 3, Track 2

Party at EWR

Terry O'Mahoney

CD 3, Track 3/4

"IF THE SHOE FITS"

Chart Analysis

"If the Shoe Fits" is based on a four-bar straight-eighth-note bass vamp figure in 4/4. Tunes based on vamps are popular with many modern jazz composers. This vamp figure appears in several places during the tune.

The proper feel for this tune is a straight-eighth-note ECM-type groove. Try to accentuate the rhythm of the vamp or melody in your ride pattern and enhance the groove with accents and fills on the snare, toms, and bass drum. After the eight-bar introduction, the melody begins at Letter A and continues until the end of letter B.

Letters C and D feature a tenor sax solo with background figures. The solo begins sparsely, so I try to focus on laying a solid groove with few fills. As the solo becomes more rhythmic and busy, I reflect that in my accompaniment. When the background figures begin, I normally try to maintain the ride cymbal pattern while "setting up" some of the background figures with the snare drum.

The drum solo from Letter E to G is played over the main vamp. I begin by clearly incorporating the vamp's rhythm into my drum solo. As the solo progresses, I deliberately move away from making obvious rhythmic references to the vamp. Playing over vamps allows me the freedom to play musical ideas "over the barline" or to stretch the pulse and return to it (which may be heard in my solo).

Letter H serves as the transition from the drum solo (Letter G) to the return of the melody (Letter I). The first bar of letter H has an ensemble figure that "unites" the entire band for a just a moment before the transition emerges to take the listener back to the original melody. I approach this section in the same way as the original statement of the melody by maintaining a strong, yet variable ride pattern that accentuates the rhythm of the melody.

Letter K serves as the coda for the tune. The guitar plays some spacy fill ideas as the bass restates the vamp figure several times, and I try to play some complementary rhythms and "colors" on the cymbals that do not obscure the light texture of the guitar. There is a slight *ritard* in the last three bars of the tune. It is important that the drums and bass feel the *ritard* together, so I often "fill" between the rhythms of the vamp to convey the speed of the *ritard*.

An example of a tune with a similar rhythmic approach is "Evanescence" on the Maria Schneider Jazz Orchestra CD *Evanescence*.

Example 28A: Use this excerpt to practice soloing over the drum solo vamp section from Letter E to G. This excerpt includes the metronome track but the play-along track does not.

CD 3, Track 5

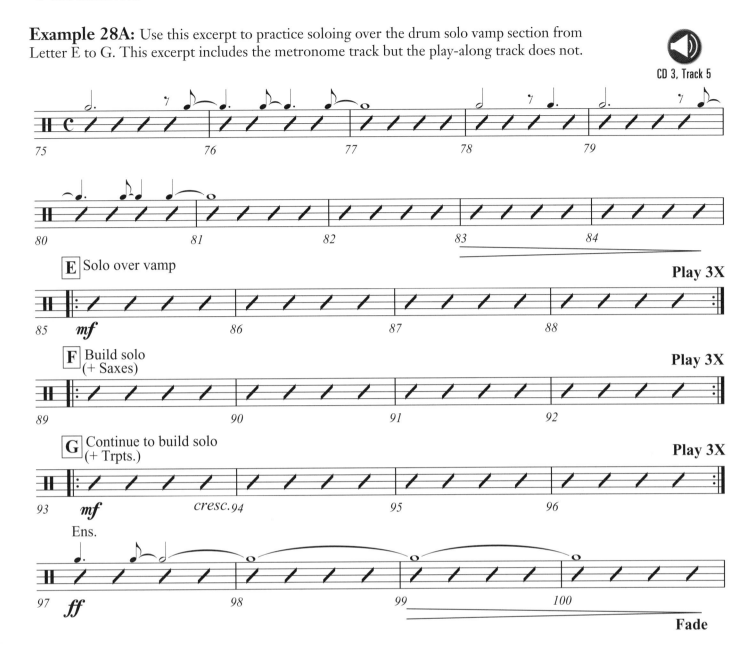

Fade

If the Shoe Fits

Terry O'Mahoney

"SANTORINI"

Chart Analysis

"Santorini" is a modern modal tune in 3/4. Like "If the Shoe Fits," it uses a straight-eighth-note ECM-style drum groove. The tune begins with a seven-measure *rubato* piano introduction. Listen to it several times, try to "feel" some type of pulse, and memorize how the last melodic fragment sounds (in this case, a single, high B-flat) so you will be ready when you have to cue the tempo into Letter A.

After the seven-bar piano introduction, the chart indicates that the drums should "set the tempo." This is usually done one of two ways: either the conductor counts it off or conducts the tempo (in a live situation), or the drummer sets a predetermined tempo alone. Either way will work. (For the purpose of this play-along, you will hear six metronome clicks to indicate the tempo for the drum intro bar in measure 8.)

The whole band enters at Letter A, and the melody is first played by the trumpets. I play a straight-eighth-note "broken ride" cymbal pattern that reinforces the rhythm of the melody from the introduction though Letter B. Letter C (played four times) is the beginning of the alto sax solo. It begins rather softly, so I primarily accompany it with cymbals. The alto solo continues at Letter D but now with a 3/4 swing feel and horn backgrounds. I try to make the tune feel like a jazz waltz and integrate the background figures into my accompaniment.

The drum solo occurs from Letter G to K, with a return to a straight-eighth-note feel. The vamp begins softly, with only the bass and left hand of the piano, so I try not to overpower them with too many notes or a loud dynamic. Each letter (G, H, I, J, and K) is played twice, with a different section of the band adding another layer of melodic material. As more of the band adds to the vamp, I begin to play more notes and louder until the resolution point at Letter L. Letter L serves as an interlude that returns to the restatement of the melody at Letter M. I play rather lightly on the cymbals beginning at four bars after L because it is a guitar solo and I do not want to be too loud.

I approach Letter M to the end of the tune the same way as the original statement of the melody, with a straight-eighth-note "broken ride" cymbal pattern that reinforces the rhythm of the melody. I play a sustained roll on two cymbals at the fermata and cut off the band with a final drum fill.

Recorded examples that are similar to "Santorini" include "Green Piece" (*Evanescence*, Maria Schneider Jazz Orchestra) and "In a Mellotone" (*Observatory*, Julia Dollison).

Example 29A: Use this example to practice soloing over the vamp section from Letters G to K. This excerpt includes the metronome track but the play-along track does not.

CD 3, Track 8

Santorini

Terry O'Mahoney

CD 3, Track 9/10

"DUTCHMAN'S OPUS"

Chart Analysis

"Dutchman's Opus" is a jazz/funk tune in an AABA form. The A sections (mm. 13–31, 44–53) are in 7/4 and the B section (mm. 32–39) is in 5/4. Letter C (mm. 40–43) is a four-bar interlude between the first B section and the last A section of the melody.

This is primarily a groove tune; the focus is on its odd meters (7/4 and 5/4) rather than on the normal job of "setting up" the ensemble figures for the band. The creative element of this tune lies in how one is able to vary the groove throughout the tune, yet keep the band together. Although I am varying my drum part, this is the basic groove that I use in the 7/4 sections:

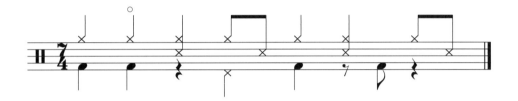

The tune begins with the four-bar bass vamp that is the foundation of the tune. A tenor sax begins a brief solo on the second repetition of measure 5, and a trombone solo is added at measure 9. The melody begins in the trumpets at Letter A, with backgrounds and countermelodies beginning after the first ending. Letter B is in 5/4, and my drum part mirrors the melody lines in the saxes and trombones (measures 33, 35, 36–39) on the toms. I re-establish the main groove at Letter C (substituting snare drum for the previous cross-stick part) and continue until letter D.

At letter D, a tenor saxophone solo begins. I concentrate on keeping the groove fairly static. As backgrounds are added (beginning in measure 62), I try to incorporate them into my accompaniment. The restatement of the melody occurs at Letter G, after the last eight bars of the sax solo. I approach this section the same way as the original melodic statement—with a constantly changing drum pattern.

Letter J (played eight times) is the drum solo over the main vamp figure. I build the solo in complexity from the beginning to the end at Letter K. I repeat some ideas, use various note subdivisions, and play some phrases that do not resolve on beat 1 of every bar to add variety and interest.

Letter K to the end is the coda, which is basically a repeated fragment of the melody with a *ritard* in the last two bars.

Examples of tunes that are similar to "Dutchman's Opus" include "Metamorphos" (*Extended Play Live*, Dave Holland), "High Noon" (*Gratitude*, Chris Potter), and "Seven Eleven" (*Unspoken*, Chris Potter).

Example 30A: Use this example to practice soloing over the 7/4 vamp at Letter J.
This excerpt includes the metronome track but the play-along track does not.

CD 3, Track 11

Drum Solo over vamp (8X)

mf   **Fade**

CD 3, Track 12/13

Dutchman's Opus

Terry O'Mahoney

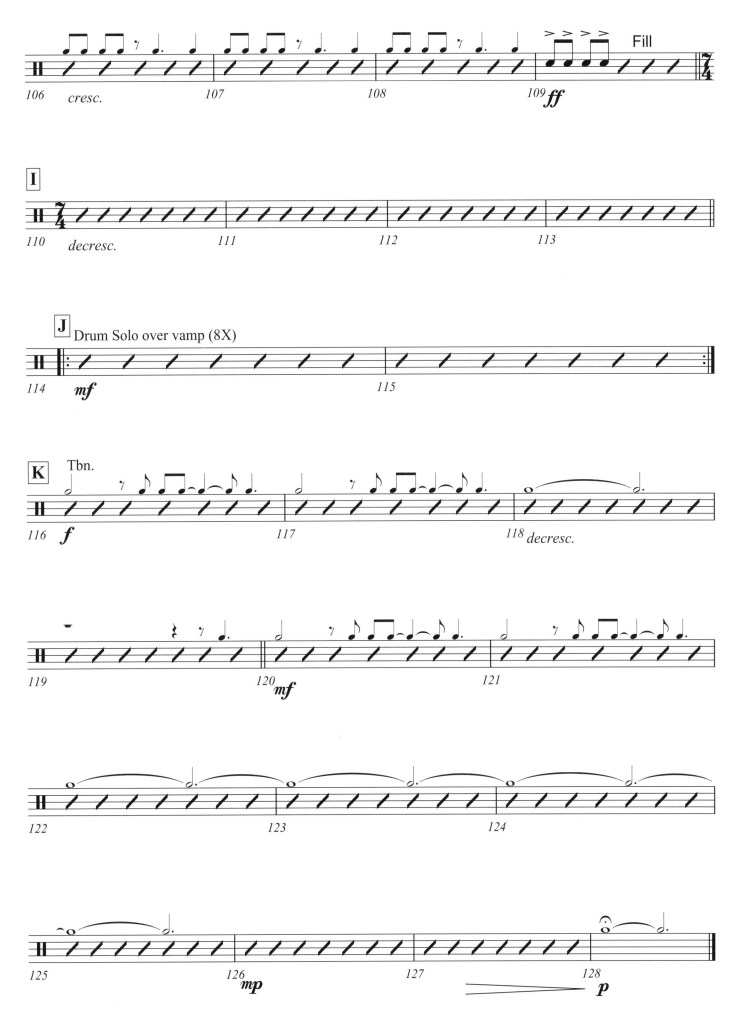

"CLEAN SWEEP"

Chart Analysis

"Clean Sweep" is a medium-fast bebop (swing) tune that incorporates a number of challenges for the drummer. It has a 32-bar AABA form with a 32-bar brush solo introduction. There are several standard tunes in the big band repertoire that require brush solo chops, so "Clean Sweep" was written as a vehicle for addressing such situations.

After the brush solo, the melody begins at Letter B. It is a fairly typical bebop-style melody, with syncopated eighth-note saxophone lines and staccato accompaniment figures from the brass sections. While playing time, I try to incorporate several of these accents in my snare drum comping (mm. 36, 42, 43, etc.).

Another common "transition" found in charts is the change from brushes to sticks, which happens at measure 64. Placing my sticks within reach *before* I begin playing the chart is the key. I get my sticks ready on a nearby chair (covered with a towel to prevent any accidental noise when I retrieve them). I complete the phrase in measure 64 on brushes, then grab a stick in my right hand and begin playing the ride cymbal on the downbeat on measure 65. After starting the ride pattern with my right hand, I place the brushes onto my bass drum shell (in case I need them later in the chart) and pick up the other stick in my left hand. It is important during this type of transition to not stop playing the time and yet make the transition smoothly.

At Letter D, the trombone solo begins. I play the background figures (using the snare for eighth notes and cymbal/bass drum accents for quarter notes or longer) on my main ride cymbal until Letter F. I switch to a smaller, quieter cymbal for the section at Letter F in order to balance with the timbre of the guitar solo. When the bass solo occurs at Letter G, I switch to a traditional hi-hat pattern for two reasons: (1) it is stylistically appropriate, and (2) it can be played softly. I don't play too many comping figures on the bass drum or snare drum during bass solos because that tends to overpower a bass soloist.

Letter H begins the drum solo, which begins at measure 129 and ends in measure 160. The drums are soloing but they are accompanied by rhythmic background figures. I wrote the rhythmic figures played by the band *above* the staff because this is the method that some composers use. The figures could have been written in the staff. The challenges of a drum solo like this one are many: to maintain a strong sense of time in order for the band to be able to play their parts confidently, to present some good solo ideas, to capture and maintain the listener's interest as the solo builds, and to make a viable musical statement.

It is important to keep in mind (as well as practice) the following concepts:

> Maintain a strong sense of time by avoiding musical ideas that confuse the band. Too many poorly executed polyrhythms or odd phrases can wreck a band in an instant. Try to "set up" the band figures as much as possible. This is especially true with a band you haven't worked with before or a group of inexperienced players. The stronger you "set up" the rhythmic figures, the more likely the band is to play their parts with conviction and ease.

> Build your solo. Begin with simple ideas and become more complex as the solo develops. You do not want to use all of your great ideas in the first two bars and then have nothing left to say.

> Use repetition, dynamics, theme and variations, musical ideas from other drum soloists, or any other solo concepts you have studied to make a strong musical statement. (Read more about these, and other, solo concepts in *Motivic Drumset Soloing*, which is listed in the *Recommended Books* appendix.)

After the drum solo, there is a *D.S. al Coda* back to Letter B (this time played with sticks) and the coda sign at measure 56. The coda begins softly with a pedal section (previously discussed in Chapter Two) before two four-bar drum breaks and a short ending. "Setting up" the band entrances in measure 173 and playing cohesive, easy-to-follow drum fills in mm. 174–177 will ensure a strong finish.

Examples of tunes that feature brush solos include "Brush This" (*Groove Shop*, Clayton-Hamilton Jazz Orchestra) and "Wyrgly" (*Evanescence*, Maria Schneider Jazz Orchestra).

Example 31A: Use this example to practice soloing around the rhythmic figures from Letter H to I. This excerpt includes the metronome track but the play-along track does not.

CD 3, Track 14

Fade

Clean Sweep

CD 3, Track 15/16

Terry O'Mahoney

"UP AND BACK AGAIN"

Chart Analysis

"Up and Back Again" is a medium-tempo swing tune containing two metric modulations. (Metric modulations were also used in Example 21 in Chapter Two.) Metric modulations can be created between any two tempos, so there are no "standard" metric modulations. I chose to create two metric modulations in which the "new" tempo is played by some members of the band prior to the tempo change (in this case, the trumpets in measure 98 and the saxes in measure 132) to make it easier to understand the tempo changes.

The challenge of metric modulations lies in relating the original tempo to the "target tempo" and accomplishing the transition between the two. A good first step in relating the two tempos is to try to indentify some sort of "pivot point." A "pivot point" might be described as the area where the "target tempo" can be stated (or heard) before the actual tempo change. In the case of the first metric modulation (measures 98–100), the *quarter-note triplets* played by the trumpets in measure 99 becomes the *quarter-note pulse* in the "new" tempo in measure 100, so measure 99 would be the "pivot point" in this metric modulation.

To make a metric modulation work, it is necessary to be subdividing the beat into the "new" (modulated) tempo *before* the modulation takes place. Seeing that the quarter-note-triplet pulse in measure 99 becomes the quarter-note pulse in measure 100, I prepare for the tempo change by playing quarter-note triplets in measure 98 (1-trip-let 3-trip-let) on the ride cymbal. As I arrive at measure 99, I continue to play my ride cymbal at the same speed and begin to count measure 99 as if it were a bar of 6/4 time (1-2-3-4-5-6). When I arrive at measure 100, I am already playing the speed of the quarter notes on my ride cymbal, so I then "switch" my counting back to a bar of 4/4 time. Note: all of the notes in measure 98–100 are exactly the same tempo! This takes some getting used to, so try counting it this way with Example 32A before attempting to play it.

Example 32A: Use this excerpt to practice the metric modulation into measure 100.

CD 3, Track 17

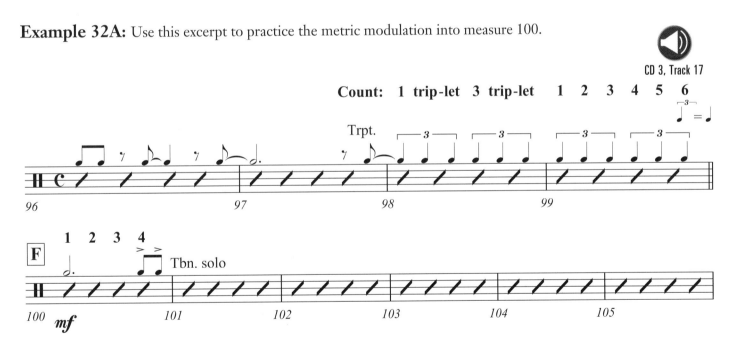

Counting measure 98 in triplets and measure 99 like a 6/4 bar (which are at the same tempo), allows me to lock in the tempo in 4/4 I need at measure 100.

Example 32B: Practice the metric modulation separately by "breaking down" the transition into measure 100 with this counting exercise:

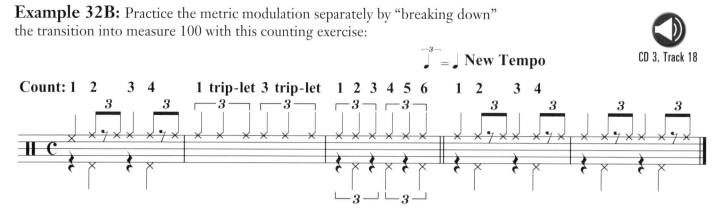

The second metric modulation occurs in measure 134. In this case, the dotted-quarter-note pulse (which is played by the saxes beginning in measure 132) becomes the quarter-note pulse in measure 134. The "target" tempo (measure 136) will therefore be slower than the tempo in measure 133.

I execute this metric modulation by counting the dotted-quarter notes (starting on the "and" of beat 1 in measure 132) as if they were quarter notes in a 5/4 bar and playing them on the ride cymbal. I continue to play my ride cymbal notes at the same speed as I arrive at measure 134. When I arrive at measure 134, my ride cymbal is already playing the quarter-note pulse (having gotten it from the dotted-quarter notes in the previous bar). I continue to play the remainder of measure 134 in the new "target" tempo.

Example 32C: Use this example to practice the metric modulation into measure 134.

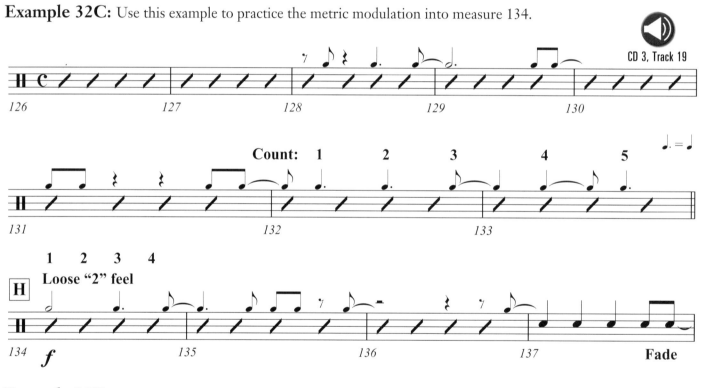

Example 32D: Practice the metric modulation separately by "breaking down" the transition into measure 134 with this counting exercise:

Some recorded examples of metric modulations include "I've Got Rhythm" (*All in Good Time*, Boss Brass) and "Wyrgly" (*Evanescence*, Maria Schneider Jazz Orchestra).

Up and Back Again

CD 3, Track 21/22

Terry O'Mahoney

"W.D."

Chart Analysis

"W.D." is a ballad composed loosely in the style of the great Bill Evans trios. The melody section begins with an implied "loose 2 feel" with a sense of swing. It soon moves to a traditional "4 feel" for the trumpet solo at Letter C. The arrangement changes to a double-time swing section at measure 69 (Letter E) before returning to the original tempo at Letter G.

The first requirement of this chart is to develop an implied "2" feel with brushes for the section up to Letter C. Listen to Paul Motian play brushes on "Gloria's Step" on Bill Evans' *At the Village Vanguard* CD or Jack DeJohnette on "In Love in Vain" on the Keith Jarrett Trio *Standards*, *Vol. 2* as examples of this feel. At letter C, you need to change to sticks to play a traditional swing "4" feel.

Other challenges in "W.D." include the transition to double time at Letter E (measure 69) and the return to the original tempo at Letter G. One way to make the transition to double time is to count 1-2-3-4 on the last four eighth notes in measure 68. By subdividing the beat in this fashion, the last four eighth notes in measure 68 will become the tempo of the half notes in measure 69 (Letter E) and make the transition to double time easier.

Example 33A: Use this excerpt to practice the transition into measure 69.

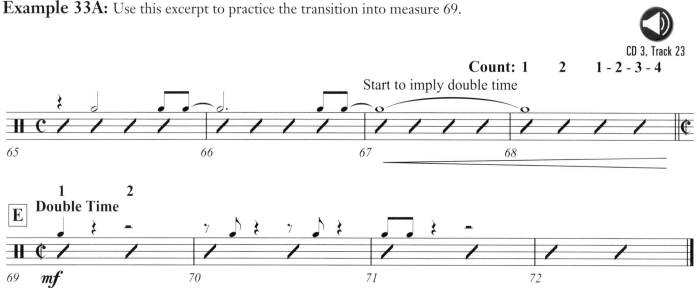

At the end of a double-time section, many horn sections have a tendency to drag and play their figures slower than the original tempo. You can avoid this pitfall by being prepared for the return to the original tempo by carefully subdividing the beats that precede the return of the original tempo.

Example 33B demonstrates how to subdivide the beats before the return to the original tempo at Letter G. Prepare for the return to the original tempo in measure 101 by counting half notes in measure 99 and 100 (1-2-3-4). By subdividing in this fashion, the half notes in measure 99–100 will become the tempo of the quarter notes when you return to the original tempo in measure 101.

Example 33B: Use this excerpt to practice the transition into measure 101.

CD 3, Track 24

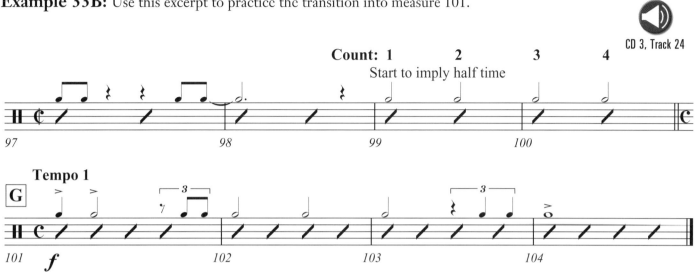

W.D.

CD 3, Track 25/26

Terry O'Mahoney

APPENDIX
GLOSSARY

These are some terms that composers write at the beginning of a chart to indicate the musical style of the chart or approach you should use when playing the chart. Often these terms can tell you more about what groove to play than the chart does. These terms can, and do, overlap.

"Broken time feel" – This could mean either a triplet-based swing feel or a straight-eighth note ECM feel. Ask the conductor or listen to how the other musicians are phrasing their parts to determine if the tune should have a swing feel or straight-eighth feel. Example 11, Example 22, "If the Shoe Fits," and "Santorini" demonstrate a straight-eighth-note feel. Example 24, "Up and Back Again," and "W.D." contain sections with a triplet-based "loose 2" or broken swing feel.

ECM feel/Straight-Eighth-Note Feel – This means to play a non-repetitive, straight-eighth-note interactive feel on the ride cymbal, snare, bass drum, and hi-hat. The pulse emanating from the drums in this style should be generated as an "overall" rhythmic approach, where the time is not created by one limb (e.g., by the right-hand ride cymbal pattern in bebop), but by the culmination of all of the limbs and parts of the drumset creating a composite pulse. This style is represented by Examples 11, 22, "If the Shoe Fits," and "Santorini."

Free – This may mean completely *rubato* (no strict tempo) or "implied tempo" where the tempo is flexible. This style is represented by the first section of Example 25. A "free" section could be played with brushes, sticks, or mallets, depending on the musical situation.

Groove/feel – These are generic terms meaning to play the specific pattern used as the basis for the tune (e.g., rock, funk, bossa nova, etc.). It is important to understand and play the correct underlying subdivision of the tune (e.g., swing feel uses a triplet-based feel, funk uses a sixteenth note subdivision, ECM music often uses an eighth-note pulse).

Latin – This is a very vague term that could mean any number of different grooves from the Afro-Cuban, Brazilian, or other musical tradition. The groove that is provided on the chart is often wrong—either poorly written or impossible to play. One way to ascertain what groove to play is to listen to the bass line to determine what groove might be appropriate. The best way for drummers to be prepared for this situation is to be familiar with many different styles of music (both bass AND drums) and choose the one that seems to suit the situation.

"Loose 2" – This term applies to the type of feel required for a tune. It normally means to play a modern, non-repetitive ride-cymbal pattern and non-repetitive timekeeping patterns in the other limbs. This style is represented by Example 24, "Up and Back Again," and "W.D." This is a generic example of a "loose 2" swing feel:

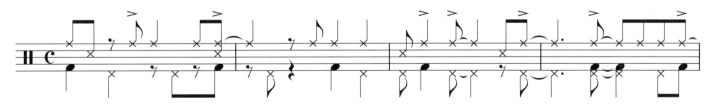

Play "colors" – This normally means to create a pulse by playing non-repetitive rhythmic figures around the drums, usually on the cymbals. This approach is requested when the composer does not want clearly stated traditional "time" from the drums but more of a texture or effect. The drums still must create some type of pulse; this does not mean play "out of time." This concept is represented by Example 25 and "Santorini."

"Play time" or just "Time" – This is a generic term that means to play the basic timekeeping pattern approach that fits the tune (as indicated by the directions at the beginning of the chart). It is also a term that is written on a chart after a drum solo to indicate that the solo is over and the drums should return to their accompanist role.

"Spacy" – This normally means to play time using primarily cymbals. Use non-repetitive figures that rely on the space between the notes as much as the notes that are actually played. Rhythmic precision is critical to this style as the listener cannot rely on any one pattern to indicate the time. Cymbal rolls are often integrated into the timekeeping vocabulary. In "If the Shoe Fits," I applied this approach in measures 27–30, 109–112, and other places where the orchestration of the chart became thin and soft and I did not want to overpower the bass line.

"Straight 4" feel – This normally means to play a traditional 4/4 jazz ride cymbal pattern. This style is represented in most of the examples in Chapter 1 and by sections of "Clean Sweep."

RECOMMENDED LISTENING

These ensembles play music that reflects some of the styles presented in this book. These recordings contain some music that is not typical big band swing music, but has more modern jazz influences or present musical challenges for the drummer. Familiarity with the music of these ensembles will better prepare you for many performance situations.

Ensemble/Artist	Recording Title
Maria Schneider Jazz Orchestra	*Allegrese, Evanescence, Sky Blue, Coming About, Concert in the Garden*
Bob Brookmeyer/ New Art Orchestra	*Waltzing with Zoe, Celebration*
Bob Brookmeyer	*Get Well Soon*
Kenny Wheeler	*Music for Large and Small Ensembles*
Danish Radio Jazz Orch/Jim McNeely	*Play Bill Evans*
Bob Mintzer Big Band	Any
UNT Lab Bands (Univ. of North Texas)	Any
University of Miami	Any
Either/Orchestra	*The Brunt*
John LaBarbera	*Fantazm, On the Wild Side*
Brussels Jazz Orchestra	Any
Neufeld-Occhipinti Jazz Orchestra (NOJO)	Any
Amsterdam Jazz Orchestra	*Finding the Way*

SELECTED STYLISTIC LISTENING EXAMPLES

Style	Drummer	Artist/Album Title
Straight 8th ECM	Jon Christensen	Ralph Towner/*Solstice*
Swing 8th ECM	Jack DeJohnette	Keith Jarrett/*Standards Vol. 1 & 2*
Odd meter jazz/funk	Billy Kilson	Dave Holland/*Prime Directive*
Rubato/Free	Jack DeJohnette	Chris Potter/*Unspoken*
	Paul Motian	Paul Motian/*I Have the Room Above Her*
Modern Afro-Cuban	Antonio Sanchez	Antonio Sanchez/*Migration*
Modern interactive	Ari Hoenig	Jean Michel Pilc Trio/*Welcome Home*
Modern Latin trio	J. Watts/T.L. Carrington	Danilo Perez/*Panamonk*
Modern jazz	Bill Stewart	anything
Brazilian drumset	Duduka Da Fonseca	Trio Da Paz/anything
World Music/perc.	Trilok Gurtu	Oregon/*Oregon*

RECOMMENDED BOOKS

These books are available for further study in their specific categories:

Jazz (Swing)

This book is excellent for developing basic jazz patterns, independence exercises, and overall jazz concepts. It includes play-along tracks for practical application of the concepts presented in the book.

The Art of Bop Drumming. John Riley (Manhattan Music)

This book presents more advanced jazz drumming concepts:

Beyond Bop Drumming. John Riley (Manhattan Music)

Big Band

These books will help develop the concepts needed to successfully interpret a big band chart. They include concepts about how to conceptually approach a big band chart, "set up" ensemble figures, and how to phrase background figures.

The Jazz Drummer's Reading Workbook. Tom Morgan (C. Alan Publications)
Inside the Big Band Drum Chart. Steve Fidyk (Mel Bay Publications)

Afro-Cuban/Brazilian

This book presents examples of various Afro-Cuban and Brazilian rhythms. The play-along tracks provide a practical way to apply the rhythms with an ensemble.

Afro-Caribbean and Brazilian Rhythms for Drumset. Drummers Collective Series. (Carl Fischer)

Stylistic Studies

This is a great play-along instructional package that presents numerous play-along tracks across a broad musical spectrum (rock, funk, reggae, Afro-Cuban, Brazilian).

Essential Styles for the Drummer and Bassist. (Volumes 1 & 2)
S. Houghton and T. Warrington (Alfred Publications)
The Ultimate Drumset Reading Anthology. Steve Houghton. (Alfred Publications)

Soloing Concepts

This book presents practical concepts that will strengthen a drummer's ability to construct cohesive drum solos and organize musical thoughts into logical musical phrases.

Motivic Drumset Soloing. Terry O'Mahoney (Hal Leonard Corporation)

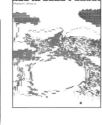